c.1

595.7 Whitlock, Ralph
WHI
    A closer look at
      butterflies and
      moths

DATE			

c.1

© THE BAKER & TAYLOR CO.

A CLOSER LOOK BOOK

Published in the United States by
Gloucester Press in 1978

Originated and designed by
David Cook and Associates
and produced by
The Archon Press Ltd
28 Percy Street
London W1P 9FF

First published in
Great Britain 1977 by
Hamish Hamilton
Children's Books Ltd
90 Great Russell Street
London WC1B 3PT

The author wishes to acknowledge
the assistance received from
Paul Whalley, of the British Museum
(Natural History), London,
during the preparation
of this book.

Library of Congress Cataloging in Publication Data

Whitlock, Ralph.
  A closer look at butterflies and moths.

  (A Closer look book)
  Includes index.
  SUMMARY: Describes the physical appearance
and habits of butterflies and moths.
  1. Lepidoptera—Juvenile literature. [1. Butterflies.
2. Moths] I. Swift, Tony. II. Weare, Philip. III.
Weaver, Norman. IV. Title.
QL544.2.W48 1978   595.7'8   77–15605
ISBN 0–531–02488–1
ISBN 0–531–01425–8 lib. bdg.

Printed in Italy
by Alfieri & Lacroix

A closer LOOK at

BUTTERFLIES AND MOTHS

Ralph Whitlock

Illustrated by

Norman Weaver, Tony Swift, Philip Weare

Gloucester Press · New York · 1978

The Lepidoptera

Micromoths

The Lepidoptera can be divided into three types. First are the micromoths, which include many common clothing and crop pests.

Moths

The rest of the moths are medium to large sized. This is an Emperor moth. There are seven times as many kinds of moths as there are butterflies.

Butterflies

Last come the butterflies, the day-flying members of the Lepidoptera. The butterflies above are White Letter Hairstreaks.

Butterflies are some of the most beautiful of all insects. Their flashing colors, their fragile forms and their complex markings make butterflies seem so delicate and joyful that they have long been a symbol of everything fleeting and free.

Of an estimated 165,000 species of Lepidoptera, however, only about 20,000 are butterflies. The rest are moths. The word Lepidoptera comes from the Greek, and means "scale-winged." This is because butterflies and moths have thousands of tiny scales covering their wings and bodies. These brilliantly tinted scales give the insects their colors. All Lepidoptera have four wings, arranged in a front pair and a hind pair. Like other insects, their bodies are divided into three sections: the head, thorax, and abdomen. Lepidoptera also have a complicated life cycle.

Although insects have lived on the earth for more than 300 million years, butterflies and moths first appeared on the scene only 120 million years ago. Yet these delicate creatures have survived far longer than man, who has been here only 5 million years. They are found everywhere except in polar regions but they live mostly in the tropics. There, the hot, humid climate has led to an enormous variety of richly colored species.

The name "butterfly" was first given to the European brimstone, whose rich color reminded farmers of the butter made from the milk of cows who had eaten young grass. Butterflies come in many shapes and sizes. In all, some 20,000 different species are known. They range in size from tiny pygmy blues barely .4 inches (a centimeter) across to the giant birdwings some 9.7 inches (25 cm) from wingtip to wingtip. Not all butterflies are colored: some are marked in dull browns and grays and have such thick bodies that they resemble moths. Sometimes it is difficult to tell a butterfly from a moth at first glance. There are brightly colored moths that fly during the day and tropical butterflies that fly only at dusk. But for the most part, moths are night-flying. Many have wide, feathery antennae. Butterflies are day creatures. Their antennae are long, slender, and knob-ended, and they usually fold their wings together upright when they land, while moths spread theirs out wide and flat. Moths also have thicker, furrier bodies than butterflies. Adult moths, like butterflies, are harmless insects. Yet because they are night-lovers, they seem more mysterious.

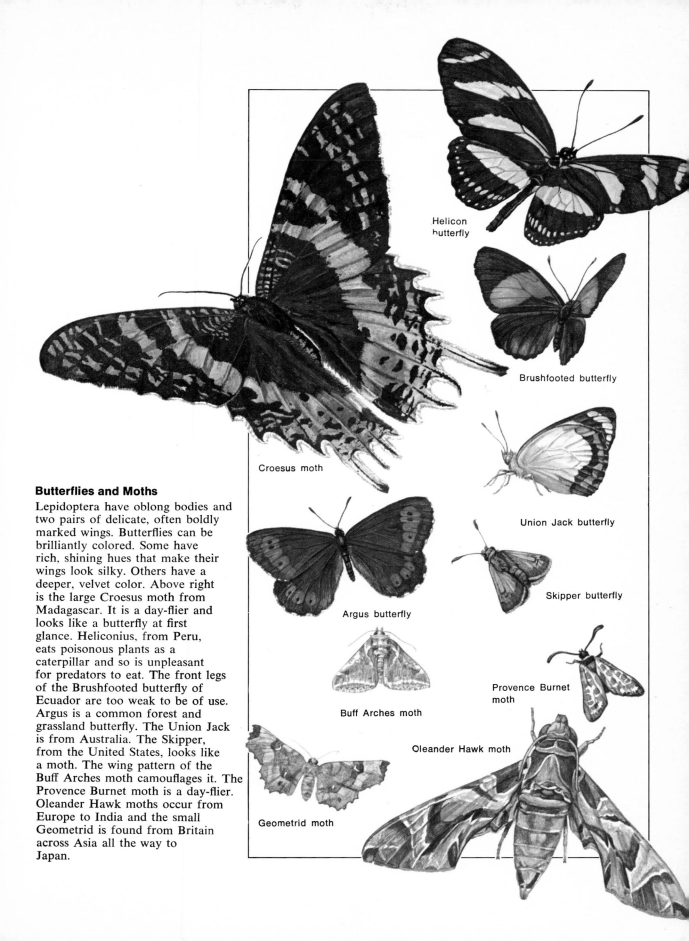

Helicon butterfly

Brushfooted butterfly

Croesus moth

Union Jack butterfly

Argus butterfly

Skipper butterfly

Buff Arches moth

Provence Burnet moth

Oleander Hawk moth

Geometrid moth

Butterflies and Moths

Lepidoptera have oblong bodies and two pairs of delicate, often boldly marked wings. Butterflies can be brilliantly colored. Some have rich, shining hues that make their wings look silky. Others have a deeper, velvet color. Above right is the large Croesus moth from Madagascar. It is a day-flier and looks like a butterfly at first glance. Heliconius, from Peru, eats poisonous plants as a caterpillar and so is unpleasant for predators to eat. The front legs of the Brushfooted butterfly of Ecuador are too weak to be of use. Argus is a common forest and grassland butterfly. The Union Jack is from Australia. The Skipper, from the United States, looks like a moth. The wing pattern of the Buff Arches moth camouflages it. The Provence Burnet moth is a day-flier. Oleander Hawk moths occur from Europe to India and the small Geometrid is found from Britain across Asia all the way to Japan.

The life cycle

The life cycle of butterflies and moths begins with courtship and mating. The males fly about looking for females. Since butterflies tend to fly in groups, they have little trouble finding each other by sight. Mating couples can often be seen on their favorite plants. Night-flying moths use smell instead of sight to find each other.

The fully grown adults bear no resemblance to the creatures they were at birth. They go through four different stages, changing their shape dramatically at each stage. They start as eggs that hatch into caterpillars, also called larvae. Then the caterpillar turns itself into a pupa, or chrysalis. Now, all wrapped up in a special coating to protect it from the outside world, it goes through a complete physical change called a metamorphosis. When the chrysalis is ready, the skin splits open and out crawls a fully formed, winged adult. Within a few hours, its wings have dried out and another butterfly flutters away.

Mating

Male butterflies, like the courting Adonis Blue (above), flutter above the female to show their interest. When mating, butterflies and moths meet tail-to-tail, like the Poplar Hawk moths (below).

Eggs

The Monarch butterfly (above) lays its pale eggs in spring along the route of its migration to Canada and the northern United States. After laying, it dies. Moth and butterfly eggs are tiny, and are often laid in huge numbers to insure that some survive. The eggs are usually laid on or under stems and leaves.

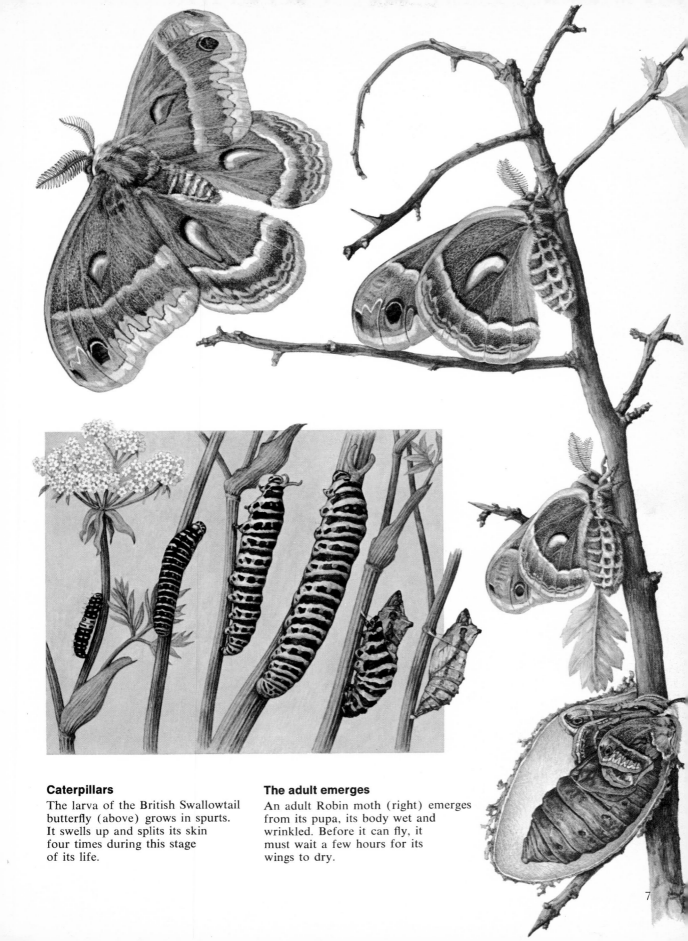

Caterpillars

The larva of the British Swallowtail butterfly (above) grows in spurts. It swells up and splits its skin four times during this stage of its life.

The adult emerges

An adult Robin moth (right) emerges from its pupa, its body wet and wrinkled. Before it can fly, it must wait a few hours for its wings to dry.

Eggs and larvae

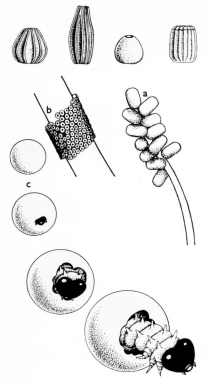

Most butterfly and moth eggs are the size of a pinhead and vary a great deal in shape from species to species. The eggs are usually white, cream, or light green when laid but darken as the caterpillars grow inside. They are often laid on plants to which they are attached by a drop of fluid. When the caterpillars are ready to hatch, they eat their way through the eggshell.

The main job of a larva is to eat and grow. It feeds hungrily on the plants around it; some will even attack wool, hair, and skins. A few larvae feed on other insects. Still others feed on fruit, seeds, grains, honeycombs, and even such manmade fibers as nylon.

Caterpillars like those of the Processionary moth are a familiar sight in southern Europe, where they can be seen moving in great columns from tree to tree. They can do a lot of damage to oak or pine trees. The larvae in turn are under constant attack by an army of predators: birds, mammals, amphibians, and other insects, like the parasitic wasps. As self-protection, caterpillars use a variety of disguises. Some conceal themselves inside leaves, imitate twigs and bits of bark, or play dead. The Puss moth relies on its scary appearance to frighten away enemies. Others spin lines of silk to bend the edges of leaves into tiny tents, inside which they feed in safety.

Eggs

Lepidoptera eggs come in many shapes and sizes. Some species, like the Kentish Glory (a) and Lackey (b), lay eggs in clusters. Others, like the Swallowtail (c), lay single hidden eggs.

The eating machine

Lepidoptera larvae are slow-moving and clumsy. Their bodies are divided into many segments that, in turn, are grouped into three sections. The head is armed with powerful jaws and complex mouthparts essential to the larva's constant eating habits. Close up, the bunch of tiny eyes can be seen. The thorax has three pairs of legs, while the abdomen has four pairs of "false legs" that carry hooks. The larva "breathes" through holes in the side of its body. Air flows through them and on into the bloodstream.

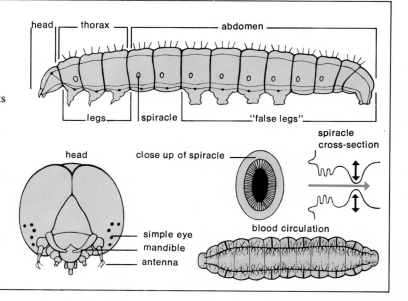

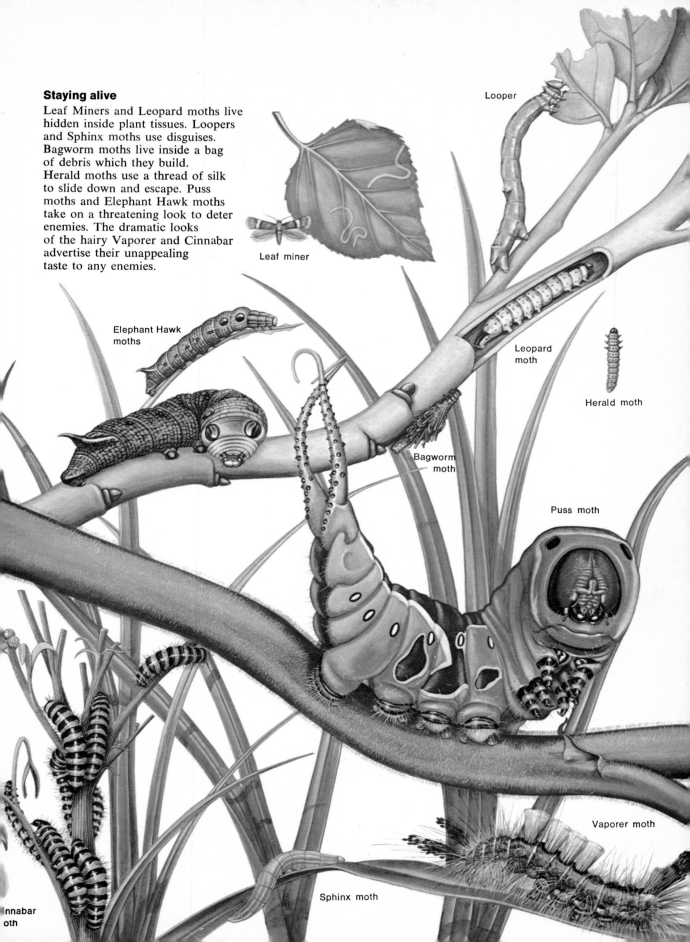

Staying alive

Leaf Miners and Leopard moths live
hidden inside plant tissues. Loopers
and Sphinx moths use disguises.
Bagworm moths live inside a bag
of debris which they build.
Herald moths use a thread of silk
to slide down and escape. Puss
moths and Elephant Hawk moths
take on a threatening look to deter
enemies. The dramatic looks
of the hairy Vaporer and Cinnabar
advertise their unappealing
taste to any enemies.

Looper

Leaf miner

Leopard
moth

Herald moth

Elephant Hawk
moths

Bagworm
moth

Puss moth

Vaporer moth

Sphinx moth

Cinnabar
moth

Metamorphosis

The change from earth-crawling caterpillar to free-flying moth or butterfly is one of the most dramatic events in nature. As the larva feeds, it grows larger and molts, or sheds its skin, four times. After each molting, it is bigger and fatter than before. For the final molt, the skin splits to reveal a legless chrysalis, or pupa.

The chrysalis is a kind of tiny operating room in which the former caterpillar is transformed. It already has all the organs inside its body from which the adult develops. First the insides of the chrysalis are reduced to a mostly liquid state. For this reason, it must have a hardy, horny casing, or shell. Although the shape of the casing varies from species to species, many are transparent enough to see the head, eyes, antennae, thorax, and abdomen clearly outlined as they are formed.

While the insect remains a chrysalis, it is almost completely still. It can only twitch one or two of its body seg-

Silk weaving

When the caterpillar of the Cercropia moth is ready to become a pupa, it spins a cocoon of sticky silken threads around itself and nearby plant stems.

Cocoons and pupae

Right, a Swallowtail caterpillar hangs down, sheds its last skin and becomes a pupa. Below from left to right are the Emperor moth (1), Monarch butterfly (2), and Orange-tip butterfly (3). At the bottom is the pupa of a Sphinx moth, which buries itself underground.

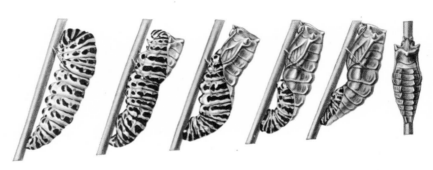

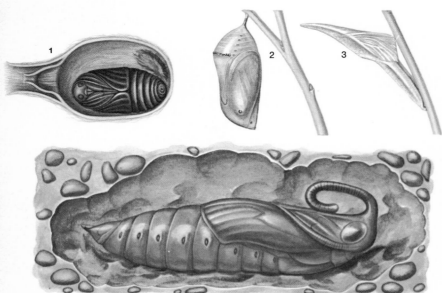

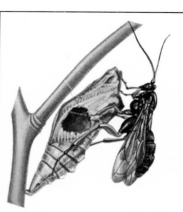

Above, an Ichneumon fly emerges from the pupa of a Swallowtail. It hatches inside the pupa, killing the larva.

ments. Since it cannot defend itself, the best protection it has is concealment. Many moth larvae bury themselves in the ground before they turn into pupae. They also have a golden-brown color, so they look like pebbles. The word chrysalis, in fact, comes from the Greek "chryos," which means "golden." Other pupae wrap themselves in silk cocoons. To an approaching enemy, the cocoons look drab and unappetizing, and the clinging silk threads tangle and are hard to get through. Pupae which stay above ground are camouflaged to look like surrounding twigs or leaves.

Some species stay in the chrysalis state only a few days or weeks. Others may spend the entire winter in this dormant condition. Eventually, however, the amazing change inside the chrysalis is completed. The shell splits open and a damp, crumpled, but perfectly formed adult insect emerges. It rests until its wings have dried and hardened, then it flies off on the last stage of its life.

The emerging adult

Above, a Peacock butterfly has just freed itself from its case and rests, waiting for its wings to dry out. Below, a Japanese Swallowtail struggles out of its chrysalis (1–3). When it first emerges, the newly hatched butterfly is weak and unable to fly until its wings have hardened (4). It is now in great danger of attack. But a few hours later it flies away, a fully mature adult (5).

A time of glory

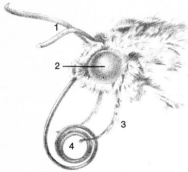

The head

A butterfly's head has a pair of antennae (1), two bulging eyes (2), a set of two labial palps (sense organs) (3), and a curled proboscis (tongue) (4). Lepidoptera have many different head shapes but the basic plan is the same in all.

The proboscis

The Sphinx moth (below) has a very long proboscis for sucking up nectar from deep-cupped flowers. Most adult Lepidoptera are nectar drinkers, though some suck up fruit and dead animal juices.

All the basic features of the adult moth or butterfly existed inside the caterpillar, merely arranged in a very different form. The large, bulging eyes let the insect see the slightest movement of lurking enemies. Lepidoptera can also see a much wider range of colors than human beings. The proboscis, or tongue, is a long tube used to suck up water or nectar from flowers. The pair of antennae are club-shaped in butterflies and feathery, or thread-like, in moths. They are important to the insect's sense of smell and touch.

The legs and wings are attached to the thorax, which is made up of three segments or parts. One pair of legs is attached to each segment. The middle part also carries the front wings, while the rear has the hind wings. The outside of the thorax is a hard casing. Under it are the muscles that operate the wings and legs. The wings are made of two flat membranes, between which is a network of hollow tubes, or veins. The wings are covered with brilliantly colored scales in overlapping layers.

The soft abdomen is half the total length of the body. It has ten segments. Spiracles—small breathing holes—lie in pairs along the side of the abdomen. Inside are the nervous system, intestines, and reproductive organs.

The body parts of Lepidoptera

The Purple Spotted Swallowtail from New Guinea sits on a branch with its wings folded vertically above its back. This is a typical butterfly position. The different parts of the body can all be clearly seen.

1. Head
2. Compound eye
3. Antennae
4. Proboscis
5. Thorax
6. Legs
7. Abdomen
8. Forewing
9. Hindwing

13

Recognition

Colors that are too bright to hide the insect still have an important function. Butterflies see in color. In the case of the Birdwings (left), the brilliant markings make it easy for them to find each other. Color helps males to identify females and makes it easier to spot other roving males who trepass into their territory.

14

The uses of color

One of the most important uses of color is recognition. Each species needs to be able to spot its own kind. Males also need to tell other males from females. Strange males are chased away. The importance of sight recognition to butterflies is shown by the fact that they can see even ultraviolet light, invisible to human eyes.

The other major use of color is as protection. When a butterfly or moth is in the air, it can usually get away from an enemy. But at rest it is much more vulnerable. Color helps to hide it when it alights. In moths, the camouflage color is on the upper side of the forewing because most moths rest with their wings flattened and the hindwing tucked under the front one. Butterflies, however, rest with their wings closed and erect. Their protective color is on both sides of the fore and hindwings.

Body color not only matches the surfaces on which the insect rests but also is patterned in blotches and designs that break up the outline of the insect and help it blend in against the background. Some moths resemble dead leaves, twigs, or patterns of light.

Other butterflies and moths make no try at concealment but get rid of their enemies by startling them. Yellow-and-black or red-and-black combinations are classic warning colors, and many species use them with great success.

Disguise
One of the major uses of color is to camouflage an insect and so hide it from its enemies. The markings of a Figure Of Eight moth let it blend into the grayish-brown bark of a tree.

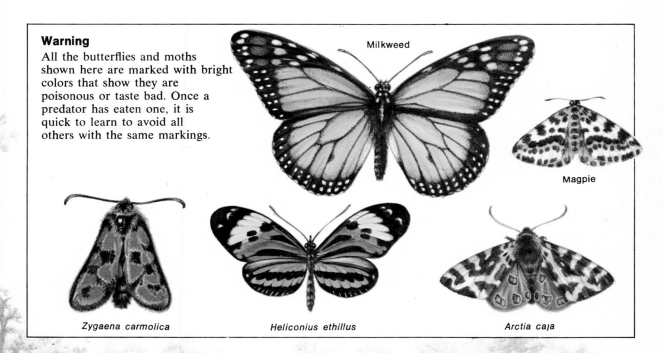

Warning
All the butterflies and moths shown here are marked with bright colors that show they are poisonous or taste bad. Once a predator has eaten one, it is quick to learn to avoid all others with the same markings.

Milkweed

Magpie

Zygaena carmolica

Heliconius ethillus

Arctia caja

The nature of color

Scales and color
Some wing scales are racketshaped, with a ragged edge furthest from the base. Others are elongated. Scales get color from their chemical pigments.

The dazzling colors that mark the wings of Lepidoptera come from thousands of tiny scales which cover the wing surfaces. The scales are positioned in overlapping rows. Each scale is really a single "cell." Its sides are flat and it has a stalk that fits into a socket in the frame of the wing. When butterflies and moths are touched, the scales rub off, leaving a fine, colored powder on the hands.

The scales have many chemical pigments. One of the most common is melanin, which makes blackish-brown hues. Other pigments give the wings white, yellow, reddish-brown, orange, and green tints. Color is not just the result of pigments. The arrangement of the scales also counts. Under a microscope, you can see that the scales are laid in long ridges. Light hitting the ridges is scattered in several directions and gives the wings their iridescent shine. As the wings move, this surface color changes in intensity. The shining blues, greens, and whites are usually caused by the way the scales lie.

Other colors are, for the most part, caused by pigments. Some scales are transparent. They give a surface shine to the wings which may range from a metallic flash to shining satin or a deeper, dull velvet. Many butterflies have both kinds of colors—the "structural" color, caused by the irregularities in the wing surface, and the pigment color.

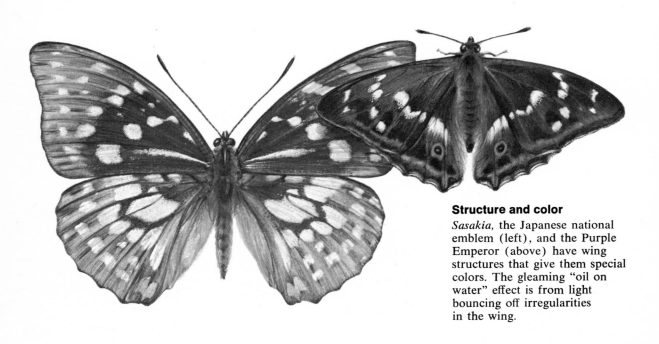

Structure and color
Sasakia, the Japanese national emblem (left), and the Purple Emperor (above) have wing structures that give them special colors. The gleaming "oil on water" effect is from light bouncing off irregularities in the wing.

Variation

In any butterfly species, there will always be variations in the colors and markings. These variations are not abrupt, but are like the varieties of hair color found in any human race. The European Chalkhill Blue is known for the range of its color variations.

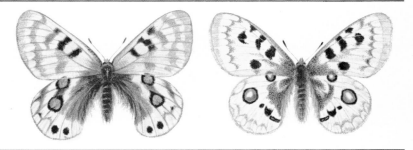

Species and sub-species

When butterflies or moths exist in isolation for a long time, some of the minor variations in markings become permanent. The differently marked race is then regarded as a sub-species. The two forms of the Apollo butterfly (right) are due to their separate environments.

Phases

The colors and sizes of butterflies can vary according to the season. Some species show dramatic changes between the spring and summer generations. An extreme example is the wet season (left) and dry season (right) markings of the African Precis butterfly.

Dimorphism

Sexual dimorphism means that males and females of the same species (here, Australian Eggfly), look different.

Masters of disguise

Like so many of their caterpillars, the adult Lepidoptera use tricks to protect themselves against attack. The large Malayan Leaf butterfly seems to melt into its background when it alights. When the wings are folded, the drab brown undersides look like a dry leaf. Although this butterfly normally alights on stems in an upright position, some observers claim it even lies flat on the ground like a fallen leaf.

Other butterflies, and many moths which spend the daylight hours at rest, camouflage themselves by means of patterns called "cryptic coloring"—mottled or striped patterns which blend with their natural surroundings. The most common form of the Peppered moth, for example, used to be light, with gray and black marks that blended with lichen-covered tree trunks. Today, the black form is the most common, especially in or near cities, where it blends well with a soot-covered background.

The "vanishing" Kallima
The Kallima imitates a withered leaf so well that it even has leaf veins. Resting on a twig, it folds its wings and seems to vanish.

Flash patterns

When a moth such as an Orange Underwing (1) is chased, the hunter watches the bright orange flash. When the moth alights (2), the orange disappears, leaving the hunter confused.

Cryptic coloring

Some color patterns help insects to blend into their surroundings. The patterning of the moths (left) blends into the bark to which they cling.

Startle effect

The boldly marked underwings of some moths surprise predators and give moths a chance to escape. The Silkworm moth has a huge "staring eyes" startle pattern (3) on its wings.

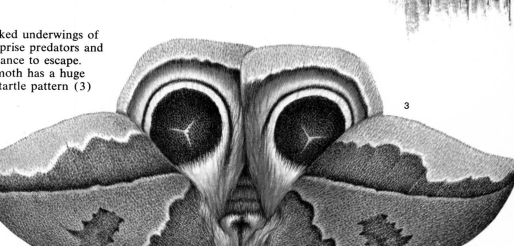

Other tricks

Mimicry is another protective device. Bees and wasps are avoided by most predators because of their stings. For this reason, some moths and butterflies imitate them. The Bee Hawk moth (4) mimics a bumble-bee. The Alcathoe moth (5) resembles a wasp. An Owlet moth (6) imitates a spider. It even goes so far as to move its large legs in a sidling motion like that of a spider. The ghost-like Cithaerias butterfly of Brazil (7) is one of a group whose transparent wings make them next to impossible to spot.

Mimics and partners

There are many examples of creatures which closely resemble each other yet are in no way related. For instance, some Clearwing moths look almost exactly like bees. This kind of imitation is called mimicry and is for the purpose of protection. One type of moth and butterfly, the model species, may be particularly good at surviving since it tastes bad or is poisonous; therefore it can fly slowly. A second species, which mimics it, may be perfectly edible. Yet by imitating the colors or behavior of the deadly species it has a greater chance of fooling its enemies. They will have learned from experience how unpleasant the model species is to eat. Any other butterfly that looks like it will also be avoided. This situation, in which a vulnerable species imitates a well-protected one, is called Batesian mimicry after the nineteenth-century naturalist Henry Bates.

Another sort of mimicry is Mullerian mimicry, named after the German naturalist who lived and worked some years after Bates. He noticed that there were often strong similarities between butterflies and moths that were equally well-protected by their poisons or unpleasant tastes. Muller pointed out that predators would therefore have to sample only one, rather than each in turn, before learning to leave all of them alone.

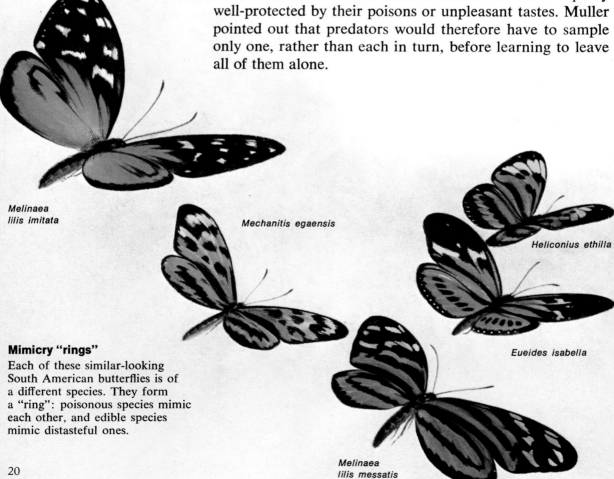

*Melinaea
lilis imitata*

Mechanitis egaensis

Heliconius ethilla

Eueides isabella

*Melinaea
lilis messatis*

Mimicry "rings"
Each of these similar-looking South American butterflies is of a different species. They form a "ring": poisonous species mimic each other, and edible species mimic distasteful ones.

Batesian mimicry

The Alcides moth of New Guinea (right) tastes bad to most hunters. Alcides is imitated by the Swallowtail, an edible butterfly. The Swallowtail mimics the flying habits of Alcides as well as its markings. The imitation of a well-protected insect by a more vulnerable one is called Batesian mimicry. It is a perfect way for an edible species to escape predators who have learned to avoid identical-looking, bad-tasting butterflies.

Mullerian mimicry

When several different species of butterflies all have the same kind of natural advantage—such as tasting bad—they may share a common set of colors and markings. For example, the Melinaea butterflies in tropical America are unpleasant to eat. By sharing their markings, other distasteful species reduce the amount of time it takes for predators to learn to leave them alone.

Alcidis agarthyrsus

Papilio laglaizei

Napeogenes apobsoleta

Hypothyris fluoria berna

Heliconius ethilla

Lycorea ceres

The butterfly day

To the casual observer, butterflies seem to flit aimlessly from flower to flower. Yet their actions are very deliberate and always have a purpose.

Most butterflies require warm sunshine before they become active. They may be seen first thing in the morning, clinging sluggishly to leaves, waiting for the sun's rays to raise their body temperatures. Like reptiles, they are cold-blooded and depend on outside warmth for their body heat. In temperate climates, they are naturally most active around midday and in the afternoon when the sun is warmest.

One group of tropical forest butterflies, the Ithomiids, have a fixed cycle of daytime activity. They visit flowers to feed in the early mornings and again in the late afternoon. Courtship and egg-laying usually occur about midday. In the heat of the day, the females hunt, examining the food plants they like for the best places to lay their eggs.

Some species adopt such rigid schedules that they may be found on the same flower at the same time every day. At night and in heavy rain, butterflies usually rest on the underside of a leaf or branch. Most species are solitary, but some gather together and sleep in groups.

22

Biological time clocks

Studies of the brightly colored
Postman butterflies of Central and
South America show that their
behavior changes in a regular
pattern throughout the day. The
butterflies roost in colonies. When
the sun wakes them, they open
their wings to bask in the warmth
(1). Then they fly to yellow
flowers to feed (2). They respond
strongly if the flowers are
swaying in a breeze. By mid-
morning, finished with the nectar
from yellow flowers, they become
interested in red. They respond to
the red patches on each other's
forewings, and males and females
begin waltzing together in the
air, getting ready to mate (3).
Having found a partner (4), they
mate in an end-to-end position
(5). When the females are ready
to lay their eggs, they will seek
the leaves of red passion flowers
on which to lay them (6). These
are poisonous, so the larvae that
feed on them will become inedible
to predators. Later in the day,
Postman butterflies return to
yellow flowers to feed (7).

A moth night

The main difference between moths and butterflies is that moths fly by night and butterflies are mainly active in the day. Those few moths which do fly by day are brightly colored like butterflies. Many of the male moths have very distinctive broad, feathery antennae, which are extremely sensitive to scent. Some males can detect females a few miles away. Although females release scent all the time, it gets lost during the day as it is carried skyward by warm air currents. After dusk, when the temperature drops, a cool layer of air forms above the ground, in which the scent "hangs," making the hours of darkness the best time for males to find females.

Many moths, like butterflies, operate on a regular time schedule. Some are active in early evening, others at dawn, and others not until late at night. Some moths fly fast and high above the treetops. Others flit slowly along, skimming the ground. Some avoid heavy rain or high winds; many do not like bright moonlight. They can see easily with their large, efficient eyes. They are sensitive to ultraviolet light and are able to see great detail. What the night woods must look like to moths, we cannot imagine. They are alive with colors and combinations of colors that we can never see.

Scent receptors

Night-flying male moths have to be able to find females by their scent. They have a pair of sensitive antennae that pick up tiny scent traces up to five miles from the female.

A day in the night

Night-flying moths feed on the nectar of light-colored flowers. They are attracted to those flowers which are strongly scented, such as the honeysuckle (below left) where an Eyed Hawk moth is feeding. But the main reason for their skill in moving at night is to hunt out mates and to breed. The Pale Tussock female on the tree (right) attracts males by scent. Moths share the darkness with many other creatures. Some, like the bat, are their natural enemies. But, just as moths can see colors invisible to human eyes, so some can also hear the high-pitched sounds of a bat, inaudible to human ears. The Noctuid moths have "ears" located on either side of the thorax and use them to detect the vibrations of the bat's signals. In the front of the picture is a Clifden Nonpareil avoiding a bat. Different moths have fairly well-defined times for flying. Some prefer dusk, while others rest until dark.

Monarch butterflies

The Monarch butterfly migrates
thousands of miles each year
from South America to its summer
home in North America. In fall,
the new generation returns south.

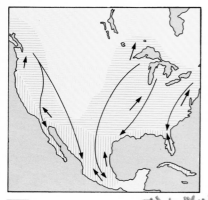

 Summer range

 Winter range

The great invasions

In spring, swarms of Painted Lady
butterflies head north from Africa
and the Middle East into Europe,
crossing the high Alps on their
way. A smaller number of their
offspring returns south in the fall.
Painted Ladies migrate because of
over-population.

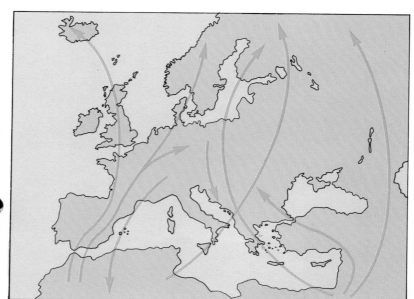

Migration

Many butterflies and moths lay their eggs in clusters, sometimes depositing hundreds in a single place. The hatching larvae form colonies on all the nearby plants. When the adults emerge, they move apart to avoid overcrowding. Butterflies generally go with the wind, but in the Northern Hemisphere, they tend to move northward in the summer.

In many temperate climates, butterflies and moths cannot survive the winter, even in the egg or chrysalis stage. The population must be renewed each spring by immigration from the south. In Europe, an outstanding example of this is the Painted Lady butterfly. Each spring, swarms surge north from the Mediterranean. Still more spectacular is the migration of the Milkweed or Monarch butterfly. Every spring, hordes of this handsome insect migrate northward across America. Their arrival is so impressive that they have become a tourist attraction and in some states are protected by law.

In the tropics, migrations regularly occur between desert and forest regions. For naturalists, insect migrations are especially exciting, as these are times when rare butterflies and moths may turn up in unexpected places. There are now techniques of marking moths and butterflies to learn more about their migrations.

Occasional visitors
Death's Head Hawk moths live and breed in southern Europe, although many migrate to northern Europe in summer.

Friends and enemies

Adult butterflies and moths are beautiful—and they do not bite, sting, or eat materials valuable to humans. But the larvae of certain kinds of Lepidoptera are serious pests. The popular expression "moth-eaten" is wrong. It is not the adult but the hungry caterpillar that does the eating. Caterpillars are enormous feeders. They also occur in such large numbers that they frequently disrupt our agricultural activities.

One of the more destructive pests is the Cabbage White butterfly. Its caterpillars feed on cabbage, cauliflower, and mustard family crops. Originally this butterfly lived in the temperate parts of Europe and Asia. But in 1887 it was accidentally introduced to North America and later found its way into Australia.

Other crop pests include the caterpillars of various moth species and certain sulfur butterflies. They feed on pasture grasses and hay, and can destroy alfalfa fields. Caterpillars do not destroy just crops. They also attack stored grain and many kinds of natural fibers.

On the brighter side of things, the Lepidoptera can be

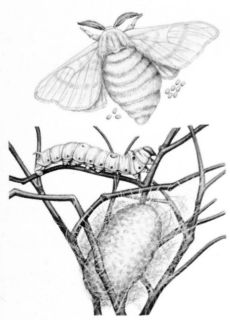

Silkworms

Silk-producing moths have been bred for centuries on farms. When the caterpillars are ready to pupate, they spin cocoons of raw silk fiber.

Pests

Caterpillars that are major pests are the Cabbage White (1), the fruit-eating Codlin moth (2), Pine Looper (3), and the Cornborer (4).

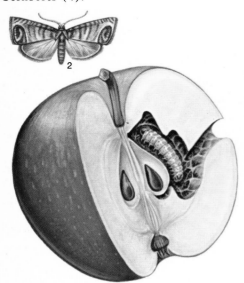

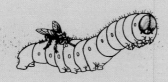
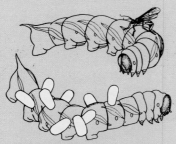
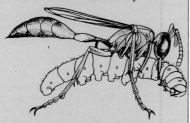
useful. The adults play a vital role as pollinators of flowering plants. Perhaps one of the most obviously useful species is the Silk moth. Originally raised in China, the larvae of this moth feed on mulberry leaves. When they begin to pupate, they spin a cocoon of silk which can be used to make a beautiful, soft, shiny cloth.

Lepidoptera are also part of the balance of nature. They feed on plants and, in turn, are a main source of food for birds, bats, reptiles, insect-eating mammals, and even other insects. Surprisingly, some of the larvae's worst enemies are ants.

Even more dangerous to caterpillars are parasite insects. Many lay their eggs next to or inside butterfly eggs, caterpillars, or pupae. When the eggs hatch, the larvae of the parasites bore into the caterpillar, where they feed on its body tissue. The Braconid wasp is a particularly fearsome parasite. The female pierces the caterpillar's skin and lays a large number of eggs inside the body. The eggs hatch and the wasp larvae feed on the fat body, eventually killing the caterpillar.

Birds
Insect-eating birds, like this
Coal Tit, are common hunters
of caterpillars.

A poorer place?

A summer without butterflies would be almost as drab as a garden without flowers. And their disappearance would be a great loss to the flowering plants which rely on moths and butterflies to pollinate them.

Lepidoptera are well equipped to cope with their natural predators. Now, their most dangerous enemy is mankind. Although in the past, greedy collectors killed countless specimens, today butterfly lovers are more likely to photograph or breed them. The real threat comes from the general destruction of their environment. Every year, thousands of acres of countryside become building projects, leaving fewer "wild places" on the earth. Without our determined effort to preserve their environments, butterflies and moths will vanish from all but the remotest places.

In the garden
In the summer, the sweet nectar of buddleia flowers can make a garden a favored place for butterflies.

Index